C000103708

PRETTY

Ahren Warner was born in 1986 and grew up in Lincolnshire. He lived in Paris whilst writing his doctorate and now lives in London. His first collection, *Confer* (Bloodaxe Books, 2011), was both a Poetry Book Society Recommendation and shortlisted for the Forward Prize for Best First Collection. He was awarded an Eric Gregory Award in 2010 and an Arts Foundation Fellowship in 2012. His second collection, *Pretty*, published by Bloodaxe in 2013, is another Poetry Book Society Recommendation. He is poetry editor of *Poetry London*.

AHREN WARNER

PRETTY

BLOODAXE BOOKS

Copyright © Ahren Warner 2013

ISBN: 978 1 85224 977 9

First published in 2013 by
Bloodaxe Books Ltd,
Highgreen,
Tarset,
Northumberland NE48 1RP

www.bloodaxebooks.com
For further information about Bloodaxe titles
please visit our website or write to
the above address for a catalogue.

Supported using public funding by
**ARTS COUNCIL
ENGLAND**

LEGAL NOTICE

All rights reserved. No part of this book may be
reproduced, stored in a retrieval system, or
transmitted in any form, or by any means, electronic,
mechanical, photocopying, recording or otherwise,
without prior written permission from Bloodaxe Books Ltd.

Requests to publish work from this book
must be sent to Bloodaxe Books Ltd.

Ahren Warner has asserted his right under
Section 77 of the Copyright, Designs and Patents Act 1988
to be identified as the author of this work.

Cover design: Neil Astley & Pamela Robertson-Pearce.

Printed in Great Britain by
Bell & Bain Limited, Glasgow, Scotland.

for Elle

ACKNOWLEDGEMENTS

Acknowledgments are due to the editors of the following publications in which some of these poems have previously appeared: *Dear World & Everyone In It: New Poetry in the UK* (Bloodaxe Books, 2013), *PN Review, POEM, Poetry London, Poetry Review, Poetry & Audience* and *The Oxonian Review* [www.oxonianreview.org]. I would also like to gratefully acknowledge the support of Arts Council England and the Arts Foundation for awards I received from them in 2012.

I would like to thank Patrick Brandon, Katie Fleming, Eleanor Irving, A.B. Jackson, Andrew Jamison, Roddy Lumsden, Fiona Sampson, Mark Waldron and C.K. Williams, without all of whom – in one way or another – this book would not take the form it does.

CONTENTS

9   Nocturne

LUTÈCE, TE AMO

13   I Here
14   II Pretty
15   III Sheer
16   IV Ennui
17   V How
18   VI Now
19   VII Pablo
20   VIII My
21   IX Between
22   X 'SO–
23   XI Between
24   XII For
25   XIII Mademoiselle
26   XIV Strange
27   XV 'However deep
28   XVI '*Vrai,*
29   XVII This
30   XVIII Before
31   XIX Thus
32   XX Having

35   Hello London
36   Ego
37   Superego
38   Four Poems after Antonin Artaud
43   As
44   *Metousiosis*
51   *Ars*
52   *Paean pro Magna Societate*

55 Kant Makes a Cuppa

56 CAPITONYMS etc.

58 *Mille platitudes*

59 Blancmange

60 'After

63 NERVOMETER

77 *Notes*

Nocturne

Between the apocrypha
of Einstein defining madness

as the same thing done over,
expecting, in effect, causation to acquiesce

and Freud, in *Das Unbehagen in der Kultur*
– that the sanest of us

has known the soft psychosis of the lover –
Biret plays Chopin,

kneads herself through him, his
injunctions

– trios played and played over –
each time a remaking, each time a submission:

a slow cloud rising, mushrooming over
a citified harbour. *Listen.*

LUTÈCE, TE AMO

Memory has no real estate... no city
where you come home and know where you are.
Is there no when
where this rampaging dream will rest?

[Durs Grünbein, 'Europe After The Last Rains']

'DÉSINVOLTE, *adj*... Showing an excessive liberty... Manner of being, of speaking, light and relaxed...from the Italian, *disinvolto*...from the Spanish, *desenvuelto*...past participle adjective of *desenvolver*...' [*Le Trésor de la Langue Française*].

'ENVOLVER (From the Lat. *involvěre*)... To cover an object partially or totally...' [*Diccionario de la lengua española*].

'IN-VÓLVERE – To wrap up, envelop, enwrap, cover.' [J.E. Riddle, *A Complete English-Latin and Latin-English Dictionary*].

I Here

the pigeons are *désinvoltes* like, I guess, the old slum shacks
    of the Carrousel were once *dis-involvebantur*,

their ramshackle awnings unwrapped, packed off, their vendors
    sent north of this *palais* wall.

Expelled I guess, like these pigeons, casual, expelling mid-air:
    piss-shit combos let fall,

land and dribble, bake and harden on the rock-hard foreheads
    of Murat, Molière and Voltaire.

II Pretty

but mad, Mademoiselle Autre had fashioned
    her accordion from a rock *des Causses*;

a block she'd found and forced from its hole
    in the wall of Philippe Auguste;

a stone she'd chipped and chiselled and faceted
    with twenty-six keys and pallets;

a boulder she'd bevelled and bound to a bellows,
    sewn from the guts of a goat.

Mademoiselle Autre, *prénom* Pierrette, stands
    on the rue Tiquetonne,

playing musette with a deft bellow shake
    (Lulu handling the *chanson*);

playing musette, melancholic, bereft, each eye
    a rest, each eyebrow a slur,

each note miasmatic, madness sublated, gifted
    like love or *variole majeure*.

III Sheer

like the young Jeremy Irons, more *Brideshead* or Florizel
    than *Die Hard*
[films have convinced us, cruelty is always theatrical],
    and camp,
desolate, at least here: younger and number than upstairs
    where,

with age, your nerves have overgrown, have blown their scales
    and you
have proliferated to a suite of selves. Now, a single exposure
    or single skin
is no longer vast or tough enough to *involvere*, to capture
    you.

And Monsieur Gance was wrong to see the hero or heroine
    resurrected
as the blessing of the silver screen, or the silver gelatin.
    There is
disintegration too, downfall and, of course, your grimace:
    a Messerschmidt

incarnate, galvanic – the brute animality of anguish.

IV Ennui

has set in for this *chimère*, so long sat between the ding-dong drone
   of Quasimodo
and Le Fantôme, whose mastery of Bach's Toccata would be more
   impressive
were it not, indeed, that it seems the only thing he knows.

So, chin in hands, this prosimian phantasm juts his mangled nose
   northwards
to where the place du Châtelet gives to Haussmann's thoroughfare
   and then
the corner of rue Blondel, a young *putain*,

Paquette, her first night on the game, fixated by those Tommes
   des Pyrénées,
Saint-Marcellins: each *involutum* in its waxen rind, waxed paper;
   all
set out to tout themselves, pimped and pressed against the glass.

At Notre-Dame, Prosimian's horns refuse to detumesce.

V How

to square the barricades, the *FFI*, the jimmying of rocks
    from boulevards –
those *appareils* of Baron H's anti-communista vistas –
    with Papon
or Pétain; the sandbags, the barbed-wire, the rifle cocked

and gripped, incongruous – a hand-me-down four-quarters
    violin
resting on the shoulder of some prodigious tot –
    and the trains
trundling out of Drancy, the *gendarmes* waving *au revoirs*.

And then, come to think of it, the only part of the plot
    of Baldwin's
Another Country I remember – Yves, I think, remarking
    that all
Americans are racists, exhibiting his Gallic *amour-propre*

and here, on the boulevard, this black woman pushing
    white tots.
How indeed. The bakers fill the street with *un parfum*
    of buttered wheat;
a pregnant beggar slumps nearby, slowly starving.

Downriver, *Les raboteurs* awaits my rapt attention.

VI Now

the cellists put their breather to profitable use, turn from Bizet
  or Vivaldi
as the violinists soar, palms toward the audience, fingers splayed,
  jazz hands
to add a little theatre to something that might be, *quelle horreur!*,
  a little exigent,
a little *grave* for this coterie from Romford, Phoenix, Denver,
  having paid
a pretty fee to pray before some crumbling saint, to hear
  this thing
they've heard so much about, that's been touted in their brochure
  as, *what's it called?*
Continental Culture... Tin Pan toccatas escape to sour the air,
  to whiff
and wisp and drift their way across the quaint medieval square,
  to brush
against the panes of Mulberry, Vuitton, Christian Dior,
  to find
their way inside the doors of Les Deux Magots or Café de Flore,
  to *involvere*
this table where, once upon a time, Monsieur Sartre would sit,
  bog-eyed,
smoking Gitanes, basking in his genius, his unfathomable wit
  just oozing
out of him. 'See here, this plaque marks a smear of intellectual
  spunk
discharged around the time he scribbled his *Cahiers pour une morale*,
  – bona fide
philosopher-cum – and yes, we have a few vials left behind the bar
  if you'd like
to take one? Every time you open the lid, it hums *Que Sera, Sera*.'

VII Pablo

Diego José Francisco de Paula Juan Nepomuceno
    María de los Remedios
Cipriano de la Santísima Trinidad Ruiz y Picasso,
    or Picasso
for short, would wander past the *garçons ou Gestapo*,

down the quai Malaquais (from the Grands-Augustins)
    and on
to the quai Voltaire, where Henri 'le garçon'
    (son of Gustave)
would greet him in his Jackson Pollock apron,

perhaps having tinkered all week with his tinctures
    to deduce
the perfect proportions of pigment to grease
    to produce
a pastel fit for Picasso's particular use,

or simply to natter over a *noisette* or *café*
    or grenadine
while, on the Grands-Augustins, Hemingway
    finds Pablo
manquant; leaves a *carte de visite*, a little *billet-*

doux: a carton of grenades, government issue.

VIII My

grandfather would never buy a poppy, would never give
    a penny
to the Legion, served his time in Burma, Sumatra,
    had
a little box of photographs I remember from the days
    after
he popped his clogs – slow death, the agony of cancer –

a photograph he took of Hirohito signing the surrender;
    others too,
more *désinvoltes*. Here, *à la tombe du Soldat inconnu*,
    Africans
tout tacky Arcs, snow globes with golden Eiffel Towers,
    key-rings,
lighters that sing the Marseillaise, posters of *La Joconde*

and, further down the Champs-Élysées, sitting slouched
    on the path,
an Arab teen, both legs spread across the gutter,
    an espresso cup
for change, skeletal, one trouser-leg rolled up,
    a limb
or stump: gangrenous, the flesh softening like butter.

IX Between

the *barre* and the *grand battement en cloche*,
　　the *en dedans*
and the *en dehors* of last night's night-off
　　fuckathon:

her room at the Grand Hotel, the *première*
　　danseuse
and me (mere *sujet*) grinding through first
　　to fifth

and on to two positions in which she led,
　　never
myself having studied – under or on top of –
　　J.G. Noverre.

X 'SO–

SO–SO', the Knights Templar would lull their *chevaux*,
   trotting
through the temple gate and on to their HQ – now a Métro –

the temple gate itself now the place de la Republique
   where,
nearby, taking a *noisette* on the rue Yves Toudic

or sauntering along, shopping for cloves or cardamom,
   I
often feel like some *chevalier*, some Templar *involutum*

in his temple mound. Faint, a mutter of *servus servorum Dei*,
   the vaguest hint
of smoke; slight tang of a smoked Master de Molay.

XI Between

the fourteenth Louis' boulevard, its tarmac lined with Acers,
    and the stage,
its sprung-floor *involutum* in Carlos Ott's *acier* and glass,
    which would have been
unknown to Monsieur Louis-Jacques-Mandé Daguerre
    whose scrubby
daguerreotype proves to be the portrait's primogenitor,
    containing –
like Brueghel's *Fall of Icarus* contains the son of Dedalus –
    the accident
of a shoe-shine boy and his customer, both motionless
    enough
to be exposed, unlike the other traffic: completely lost,
    scurrying
away and down the boulevard, towards the Austerlitz.

The shoe-shine boy and his customer and, not to forget,
    the couple
at the table sat, like we sit: principal dancer and subject
    mulling over
our Americana breakfast – my idea, attempting to emit
    a sense of adventure –
sensing that you've grown tired of my inability to master
    positions
six and seven; that last night you were thinking not of *moi*
    but
of Serge Lifar. Between us – like the thirteenth Louis' *mur* –
    this syrup made from Acers.

XII For

I will consider these kittens of Bercy, each a *servus*
  servorum
Dei, though none would stoop to serve
  nor
have any Lord before themselves.

True Epicureans, apostles of Dionysus;
  kittens
in togas, touting the grace with which they curve
  their bodies.
Each motion revelatory, a rapture, *un triomphe du Soi.*

XIII Mademoiselle

Thèse has Monsieur Antithèse rapt in the undulation
    of her *arsis*
kai thesis, the rise and fall of her intonation,
    the syrup
of her accent, the diphthongs that seem mined
    from some
wet depth, some soft and syrup-sticky inside.
    She
can feel his hands tighten around her arse,
    can smell
his eau de cologne, the static pooling on his skin.
    In the mirror
she watches herself, Antithèse an incidental closing in.

    And
Monsieur Antithèse knows Mademoiselle Thèse
    is wrapped
in his anecdotes, his wit, the perfect angle
    of his jaw;
he can sense her ankles becoming their own tangled
    knot
of tension. He can feel her flanks harden
    as she pushes
herself towards him. Behind her: flowers in a vase,
    a mirror
gilded and glistening with the thrill of his own reflection.

XIV Strange

how they lurk, these bastions of public health: the tower
   of the Temple,
the Templars turned out, the Bourbons interred,
   attendant
on the block or some infernal exile; Latvia, Edinburgh,
   again
the rise to power, the mob's rising anger, the fall.

And *La prison de La Force*, now little but a plaque, a wall
   on the corner
of rue du Roi de Sicile and the rue Mahler,
   where
the Princesse de Lamballe was gang-raped
   and lynched
by a mob *involutum* in their revolutionary fervour.

Strange too, this wall the length of the boulevard
   Arago
– bulwark of surety, blank menace, *un monument
   à la santé* –
its pluriform wrongdoers: a wronged Apollinaire,
   the occasional
evil, rare absolute; one *Monsieur le Préfet* Papon.

XV 'However deep,

this is no river of the dead or Lethe', or Rubicon,
    but a vast
and writhing cat we fondle our way along

to where the arches span, the *clefs de voûte* are set,
    the abutments
wade or bathe, to where the *pont*

straddles, struts, pontificates between the Rive
    droite
et gauche, to where the river takes its leave

of Paris, passing the last in that long *histoire*
    of walls –
the Périphérique, heir to those of Charles Valois,

Philippe Auguste, Louis 'the just' – a scrawl
    of tarmac,
beyond which the Seine stretches its paws,

flounces its tail, licks its lips and arches its back,
    skitters north.
Elsewhere, others sleep, slumber on the banks

of the Rubicon, the Nile, the Med, the Chott
    El Marej,
while we leave Javel, bus it to the pont

de Bir Hakeim, to *pontificare* how Fernand Léger
    is way too *lite*;
to hold, to *involvere*, each other beneath *les nuages*;

knowing, that for us, 'there will be sunlight'.

XVI 'Vrai,

Fernand Léger est si... *trop* léger,
   mais
Soutine met l'*a* dans l'alètheia.'

XVII This

photograph of us, two teens on our second time up
    the Eiffel Tower;
the camera *nos involvit*, has snared the coruscation
    of your hair,

the haze of early light. Our first ascent, two *crépuscules*
    before –
our first night here – having taken the bus,
    the RER

from a hotel *nord des Batignolles*, where now we'd know
    not to venture
after *crépuscule*. Those four days, this city the paragon
    of *étranger*,

now our home, our homely *involvendum*, this city
    where
we take a promenade through the *parc* or Champs
    de Mars,

the Tour Eiffel no longer notable, no longer noticed,
    another
trap for hazy tourists. I note the coruscation
    of your hair.

XVIII Before

Soutine had left Smilovitch, had left Minsk, had left Vilnius.
   Long
before Soutine had left Paris, left Céret, had left Paris
   again,

before he had left Champigny, slept rough in the forest:
   a Jew
and Slav, trying to avoid his *billet simple* to Auschwitz.
   And,

therefore, even longer before his haematemesis,
   the blood
chucked up, the ulcer that ruptured, the peritonitis,
   the covert

agony of a night-time drive, northwards, towards Paris;
   the success
of avoiding the Gestapo. Thus, long before Soutine's
   exsanguination:

the *bobo* idyll of *Le Bateau-Lavoir*, its half-starved artists.
   Et après?
Matisse, radiance of crêpe, cancer smarting like a bitch.

XIX Thus

the future, and history, belong not to the warlord,
   the master
who dies, or pickles himself, as his own
   doppelgänger

but belong to the slave, the labourer, this latter
   who transforms
the world by his work, who transcends the given,
   surpasses

himself, his self that is given, surpasses the master
   tethered
by inertia to the Given. For, if the angst of death
   embodied

in the Master is the *sine qua non* of all history,
   all progress,
it is only the toil of the Slave that can render
   it faultless,

can bring it to realisation, can realise its absolute
   perfection.

– after the French of Kojève's *Introduction à la lecture de Hegel.*

XX Having

watched a man throttled near to death, heard
    his attempt
to retch, to reach a scream, the flail of vocal folds
    failing
to find sufficient breath. Having felt the 'jolt'
    which sends
me back to where a stoned nut-job
    cackles,
his laptop hooked to an amp: the near dead
    gurgle-gasp
of a man in surround-sound, just-off beheaded.

    Having
traversed the boulevard, the *chinoises* hookers;
    walked
past this kid, gaunt, hunched below the portico,
    dealing
smack or base, I come to my shanty studio
    to *involvere*
this little étude of you – that Egon Schiele pose –
    inadequate
to him, forever inadequate to you.

Qu'est-ce que l'art pur suivant la conception moderne? C'est créer une magie suggestive contenant à la fois l'objet et le sujet, le monde extérieur à l'artiste et l'artiste lui-même.

[Charles Baudelaire, 'L'art philosophique'.]

If something is to stay in the memory, it must be burned in: only that which never ceases to *hurt* stays in the memory.

[Friedrich Nietzsche, *On the Genealogy of Morals*]

Hello London

Just as, shifting the Double-Gauss a notch, the clarity attained is not
   what appears, but how what appears does,

so *l'étranger* is not this man in the window just off the Euston Road,
   but rather a shifting in this me that is.

And, what held for Louis holds true for me. In my teens, you were
   'foreign names over winking doors';

marred, perhaps, but only by the Thames' mean gust, slate-stolid *réveil*,
   that bite I came to need.

Still, it's been years since I came to you, a little less since you began
   to nibble, then gnaw, then masticate.

I don't know if I got out, or was spat. But, somehow, I'm back: transient,
   for now; a fleeting whiff;

amuse-gueule; faint stirring of your parotid. Soon, I promise to be
   here – at your leisure, to lick and lap –

your spittle shiver now blain, now numb dread.

Ego

His right hand scores a gull-wing door
in his left *flexor*
carpi radialis, with surgical precision
and a rusty bodkin.

His right thumb delves, then runs
– a spatula
between a pancake (or *crique* or farl) and pan –
along the ulna.

He's peeled his gull-wing back
– a hunk
of belly pork – tugs, cajoles or rents
until he's stripped the lot.

He winds his veins
to bundles, hangs them on a hook.
He works
his bones with a micro-plane.

Marrow pools, then seeps away.
Through a fine, grey dust...

Superego

Somewhere in a town
in which you've never been
my fist abuts your face.

Through a fine mist
you steal the flit
of your – now *my* – gait.

Four Poems after Antonin Artaud

I

[*Poète noir*]

Black poet, an unsucked tit
haunts you. Bitter poet:

life boils, the town burns,
the sky assimilates itself in rain.

Your pen scrapes against
the heart. Forest, *forest*,

the eyes team with cogs;
poets straddle horses, dogs.

Eyes rage, tongues turn;
the sky floods nostrils as succour,

milk, blue. Women
I hang on your mouths, your

hard, vinegar hearts.

[*Les poetes lèvent des mains...*]

In their hands the poets raise
acid – alive and tremulous.

On the tables the idol-sky
braces itself... A dainty

cock dips its ice-
tongue into each stead

surrendered by the sky's advance.
The ground is bunged

with souls and women
with pretty vulvas, bantam

cadavers
            unfurling mothers.

[*Avec moi dieu-le-chien...*]

Our bitch of a god has withdrawn
from this dry socket of a language.

II

The sex street's aroused
the length
of its crumby facades;

cafés purl abuse,
uproot
the avenues.

Sex-hands broil
in pockets.
Thoughts all caterwaul:

the heads
less
than the holes.

III

The tree, its tremor, the sombre forest
of calls (cries) savours the night's

heart. Vinegar, milk, sea and sky,
thick mass of firmament conspire

to this shudder, this thick umbra.
A croaking heart, a hard star

split and fused with the sky
that cleaves itself with the cry:

the sun's clarion. It makes
the same noise, *makes the same noise,*

as tree and night at the gut's crux.

IV

This revelry hitches ponds to astral freight,
the stars' capricious plenty, our glitzy thoughts;

somewhere between the earth and sky
discards the souls' junk, which nobody

(among the burning night) sees as swans
in flight. We – muted attendants

of our own bones' transformation – regard
our brightest dreams becoming void.

As

the bow's fricative brims,
   brings back
the scent of rosin,

that scrub behind the concrete
   courts,
a generator's sibilation,

the myrtle green of wire fences,
   will all
and always smell of resin.

Metousiosis

Look, sometimes it happens my hands become aware
of each other, or my worn out face seeks shelter
in them. Then I feel a slight sensation.
But who'd dare to exist just for that?

RAINER MARIA RILKE, *The Duino Elegies*, 'Second Elegy'

[*L'avocat*, 1866]

As, between Delphi and Thebes, where *ramus*
turns to *ramuli*, old Oedipus shafts Laius

good and proper, batters him with his staff
then finishes the King (and his coterie) off...

And as, leaving the codger dead at the road's crotch,
he never looks back or gives it a second thought

but, instead, makes his way to Thebes, to years
of plenty, to night after night of shafting his mother

(that is, until she tops herself, until he digs
his own eyes out)...

        So, you happen upon your leg
or arm, and your flesh is *unhomely*: a waxed rind,

a terrine of silt and scud.

[*Sitzender männlicher Akt*, 1910]

'... the stain of blood makes shipwreck of our state'
slips drowsily into 'shipwrecked in this sea is sweet

to me'. The night presses through the shutters' slats.
Parasomnic, one finger skims the sternum's flat

then draws an ellipse from plexus to armpit
and back; arcs off and up to circle my upper lip.

So many nights I wake to find myself like this,
tracing the contours of my self – near catatonic –

one hand puppeteered and seeking the spots
where nerves hustle or a coarse down bristles;

where, beneath the glaze of *cogitans*, touch
can trigger surety – flesh and bone assurance –

    beyond this party trick of intellect.

[*Le boeuf écorché*, 1924]

And sure, who could miss the significance
of Rembrandt's *Le Boeuf écorché*, his cow carcass

strung up, crucified, painted on its stand?
The word became flesh, made his dwelling among us

etcetera. Except, as Soutine knows so well,
there is no *logos* here; the muscle and sinew

sag silently. There is only flesh and shadow,
a hush of bone, wilting skin and gristle.

The same silence throbs in Soutine's rendition
con fuoco (as Rembrandt's nose also throbs

in that self-portrait, puce and drink-pocked).
The carrion insists, exists as affirmation,

as a reverie of flesh become flesh become fleshy.

after Baudelaire

Darling, do you remember that sweet morning
down a shortcut for fear of fair-weather tourists

we came upon a carcass rotting, its legs spread
like an easy girl, nonplussed, gut swollen, stinking?

The sun beat down, blazed radiant, as if to roast,
to serve it up in its own pustulant dripping.

The bleary sky watched the carrion blossoming,
maggots pooling among tattered jerky, dry crud.

A bitch eyed us, skulked and slathered. Not if
but when, my solace, you too end up like this,

then tell the grubs and parasites that kiss
and nibble at your face, I've vouched safe

the form and essence of our love.

[*Study after Vélazquez's Portrait of Pope Innocent X*, 1953]

Amaranthine aubergine coccineous coquelicot
cardinal ponceau puccoon magenta lateritious

puniceous maroon umber madder nacarat
cinnabar stramineous vermilion miniaceous

gamboge badious kermes pyrrhous cramoisy
erythraean haematic mazarine ferruginous

sanguineous modena phoeniceous burgundy
rufous rubiginous claret incarnadine crimson

spadiceous testaceous rubious russet ruddy
vinaceous titian sorrel wallflower minium

piceous scarlet vinous sinopia solferino lurid.
Between the tongue and the *lingual frenulum*,

a kaleidoscope of red.

[Head of J.Y.M. II, 1984-85]

The same raised head, same elegant carotid
– bared and throbbing – unite both Jocasta

swinging from the rafters and lying on her bed
(*Tyrannus* and *huios* grunting on top of her).

As indeed, years later, her rebellious inbred
of a daughter

would prove again, ad-libbing a gibbet
from the sturdiest stalactite on offer

(which is not to mention her betrothed,
who undid the knot of his own cricoid

with a kopis, his carotid a fury-fuelled geyser).

Il y a si peu
            entre la petite et la pénible...

[*Nice 'n easy*, 1999]

If, occasionally, I admire my arms, my flanks,
my shoulders and buttocks against the shades,

what, before the bathroom mirror, more often
stares back, is this grotesque: soft and fault-riven.

This flesh and hair, this creased hotch-potch
of freckled fat, bulging and bobbing and blotched.

Between those strange, uncommon, fantasmatic
moments and the everyday, the chronic

shame, as each garment is yanked off or falls,
there are times like these, between your legs

(yes, like the handles of a red wheelbarrow)
where your balmy skin improves my own;

there is *this*, our sweat-glazed *metousiosis*.

Ars

(for P.B.)

Right now, I have no time
for painters
whose paintings are not

fetishes, skin flakes;
an itch
to slow, hard fuck the paint

(to slot their cocks
into Michael Harding tubes
or take
such tubes' protuberances into them).

Hypersarcoma, writes Mael Dúin
and I hark back
to Cobain:
I wish I could eat your cancer when you turn black.

Paean pro Magna Societate
(for S.O.B.)

How shall the plow   be kept   in the hands

> *of owners not hirelings?*

Seems to be the question

> they've been asking for ages

or   having solved it

> tweaking it for each new age:

from 'patrician and plebeian'

> to minimum wages

via tales of heaven   and brimstone

> or plague.

So

> last night I was reading a bio. of Auden

a paraphrase penned

> by some populist sage

> *Auden fought Franco*

> *lost his strength of conviction*

> *left Britain*

> *cared more for Britten*

> *moved to Brooklyn*

> *wrote an Opera*

> *nobody would commission*

and *yes*   I too

                have been quite   the Marxian
standing   on grim

                Garden Town   high-streets
waving leaflets   banners

                    the odd catchy slogan
and once   ardour in decline

                   watching anarchists
from a window

        CIRCA   or Black Block

                   lobbing bricks
[one eye on Trager and Smith's   *Outline of English Structure*].

Yet

       though I know the kick   of comradeship
as a Chinook   quivers

                   then lands

and the pigs come at you

            with teargas   and nightsticks
somewhere

       between that salt-and-sulphur hinterland

and now

       I've begun to hope less   for revolution
and more for a space:

       book filled and paint tanned.

Which

      of course   is not to say I'm not still prone
to upend   and scatter

       a shelf of Walnut Whips

in anger:

                                            stricken

by the news

                I live   in a country of fuckwits

or with enough to elect

                    the party of draconian pricks

[by which

                    I mean Little Lord Tory-tit].

                                          O

the chorus sings

            Rule Britannia!

                    as it's right-royally shit on.

Though

                  perhaps it proves the old adage:

At twenty

            not to be a socialist   *is heartless.*

At twenty-six

            get your shit together and get out of Albion.

Kant Makes a Cuppa

(for C.K.W.)

A pelt of cloud makes concrete of the sky,
    unfurls itself, girds

the sublime. The grey, though, is Georg's
    Unendlichkeit.

    So too the gray
horses, in your poem for James Wright.

CAPITONYMS etc.

As often as it seems a social imperative, I've never
   stooped to master

your kind of nuance-fleeced drinks party digest
   of Slave and Master.

Confronted, on occasion, by the Giant of Ljubljana,
   I fail to feel other

than a little deflated (by his fast-food induced swelling,
   his elevation to 'big Other').

Beered-up on Batesons or Muldoons: 'is it so hard
   to tell the difference

between ten-a-penny tenure-track deconstructionistas
   and the sucker-punch of *différance*?'

Underground, between Bethnal Green and Holborn,
   I altern:

'blasted' tanks to page three tits; smug monosyllabics,
   a shrapnel-rent Subaltern.

On Little Turnstile, one never – repeat *never* –
   asks for Absolut

but for Jarzebiak, Zacheta or caraway Kminkowy,
   the pedigree of which is *absolute*.

Smashed and stuttering, I experience first hand
    the ne-

gative consequence of explaining why *what's-his-name's*
    no more than the *ne*

explétif. Cue expletives. Cue one of those
    too many

hungover mornings where the pain dices the ego,
    plates up a paranoiac Many.

A weak sun rises, I'm on my knees and grabbling
    around the one

room we rent, trying to locate my *trait unaire*,
    my *einziger Zug*, my One.

Mille platitudes

As Hegel would have it:
what lies beyond your grasp

is not the infinite, but an affidavit
that you are, in fact, a dumbass.

...and no, Madame le Professeur,
the responsibility of this thesis

is not ultimately to the thetic
but to its own inevitable failure

which is not, indeed, a paradox
but proof *que je suis une pute*

and will, given a modest grant,
spend three years sucking cock

or, as you prefer, writing a doctorate
that has no more to do with art

than the burger-flipping alternative
has to do with a *consommé de boeuf.*

Blancmange

Note   how the bald   so often trawl
their fingers   through their long-lost hair

how each digit skims   its own reflection
as if their follicles   were mourning

the skull's lacquer   an oily grief   and they
consoling them.   And if

with a full head instead   I trace
each ridge and dint   until

I find the slight imperfection   where
the fontanel   once knitted itself together

and with a knuckle   or tip   dig
until the thick   bone   gives...

How I'd hope   for 'The End'   to turn
on more   than an egg-shell metaphor:

the moist surprise   of blancmange
fissuring   as it tends to

      when you stick it   with a fork.

'After

great light must be
great shadow,

which we call repose',
respite, the rest,

the silence
into which

the note
– gifted –

bleeds, until
the *nihilo* itself

becomes the gift:
sweet nothing

involutum
in intent.

NERVOMETER

After Antonin Artaud

I

I have always been struck by the obduracy
of mind – by how it must always want to think

in dimensions, in space, arbitrarily – struck
by the fixation of being with beginning...

I admit of an intricately wrought soul –
brimstone, phosphoric – as the only acceptable

mode of reality. I do not know what unknown
clarity, unnameable, gifts me this scream,

this pitch, this possibility of feeling my mind...
I would like you to imagine a state, motionless:

a mass of mind, part-buried, potential. You see,
through a crystal, an actor tread inspiration.

You must not admit too much literature.

II

I've aimed no further than the soul's automata,
transcribed no more than the sorrow of adjustment

aborted. I am a complete abyss. Those that believed
me capable – of a sorrow complete, beautiful sorrow;

an angst corporeal, replete; an angst that exists
as objects, a luminous pestling – not a point

suspended (yet, restless, deracinating needs come
via tussle of force and void, absolute end

and there is no more than these voluminous
voids, the immobile, cold), those who have given

more life to me – have thought me less fallen,
believed me plunged into torture, noise, darkness

and struggling – are lost in the shadows of men.

III

Sleep: nerves tense the legs' whole length,
myoclonic belief. The pressure eased, absurd...

We must understand, intelligence is no more
than a vast eventuality. And that it can be

lost – not like the dead, estranged, mad –
like the living, feeling its attraction, its breath

(intelligence, not life). The thrill of intelligence,
the sudden inverse of opposites, the words

nearly near intelligence. This possibility
of thinking in inverse, of sudden repulsion,

of turning invective on thought. This dialogue
in thought, the absorption, the rupture.

The trim fall. The mind, idling...

IV

To think without the least rupture, the pitfalls,
those sudden vanishings I'm so used to, which

my marrow is used to: cathodes. My marrow
flirts, sometimes, with these furtive abductions,

amused. One word would suffice, sometimes –
a simple, small word – to rise, to reach

prophetic inflection. A word – precise, subtle –
a witness soused in my marrow, a word

which would leave me, stand at my bounds:
nothing for the world. I am the witness,

my only witness. This crust of words, low voiced,
imperceptible mutation of thought: preformed,

miscarried. I am the only judge of its import.

V

Under my crust of bone and skin (skull),
there is angst, constant; not moral, not the absolute

end of deduction, of dim finickiness, or
the inhabiting of angst rising to its height, its meaning,

but a decanting at my core, the self-deprivation
of substance, vital, the physical loss, essential

– I mean the essential loss – of meaning...
...The difficulty is of finding its proper place,

of rediscovering communication with 'self'.
All this is flux, specific, of things; the reassembling

of mental cement, stone, gem; the rendering
around a point. There you go, *ego*, what I think

of thought: inspiration exists...

VI

...there is a point, phosphorescent, where reality
finds itself, though changed, metamorphosed – by what?

A point where the use of things, objects, is magic.
I believe in kamacites of the cerebellum, personal

cosmologies, dear friends. That which you have taken
for my work was excrement, scuzzballs of the soul,

which your average man would not welcome.
My illness, since then, has receded, advanced;

the question is not there, but in the sorrow, death
that persists in my skull... To return to M...

Where I recovered numbness, vertigo, this gruff
need, mad slumber, sudden loss, impotence, vast

sorrow, instantaneous numbing of mind.

VII

Life is a point. The soul is without sections, segments,
without stratification. The mind does not begin... I am

a numbnut – suppression of thought, malformation –
made vacant by language, stupefied. Malformation,

mal-agglomeration of a critical mass of glassy, glazed
cells; cells you use blithely, unknown, inattentive.

These terms I choose for thought are, for me, terms –
a precise term – true terminations of mind, ends

of states submitted to thought. I am localised, truly,
by my terms: cerebral invalids. I am paralysed

by these terms, a suite of terminations. I can think
only in terms – oxymoronic, parallel, equivocal –

under pain of stopping, halted at a moment in thought.

VIII

If one could only taste the abyss, the nothingness,
could lie down in it; if this nothingness was not

a certain living; if it was not, not completely, death.
It is so hard to be, to not be within... True

sorrow is feeling the self and, within it, this
displacement of thought, though, at a point,

thought is not suffering. I am at a point
where I can no longer touch life, though

I have all the appetites, the insistent arousals
of being... In each one of these movements

there are holes, haltings. Not in time, understand me.
In a particular kind of space, I understand me.

I mean neither extent, nor duration.

IX

I mean a thought, one, a single thought
interior. Not a thought such as Pascal's, not a thought

philosophic. A thought obsessed, skirting: a certain
sclerosis. I consider myself in all my minutiae.

I have my finger on the flaw, fissure, tectonic fault;
its secret slippage. For, the mind is more reptilian

than you, sirs, it strips itself, sheds, wrongs itself
as language, suspended. I have felt best this splayed,

stupefied language, the disarray of uttered thought.
I have pinpointed best the intimacies, its subtle

slippage. I lose myself in thought as a dream,
true. I realise my submission in thought.

I know best the nooks, these crannies of loss.

X

All writing is dishonest. Folks that shun the nebulous,
that aim to detail the events of thought, are bastards.

All men of letters are bastards, contemporary bastards
are the worst. All those who would map the mind,

all those who are masters of their language, all those
for whom words have a meaning, for whom heights

exist in the soul, currents in thought, those minds
of their times, those who have named such thoughts,

have toiled for precision, those unoiled movements,
squeaking, disgorging their minds, are bastards.

Those for whom a word has a meaning, a manner
of being, for whom feelings can be classed, classified,

discussed by degree, are the worst of all bastards.

XI

No works, not of language, of speech, of mind, nothing.
Nothing except, perhaps, a beautiful nervometer...

These states, eminent situations of the soul, these intervals
of mind; these failed letters, my quotidian pain; people,

unreal data. Always the same words that serve me, truly
there seems to be so little movement in my thought,

though more than in yours: pertinent bastards, masters
of false verbs, serial novelists, ruminants, scourge

of my language. That I no longer have language is not
a reason for you to exist, persist, insist in language.

I will be understood by a future you, a future
mediocrity. These, my salvos, will be understood;

they will have learned to understand, to discover.

XII

My hair will be cast in lime, so too my cerebral and choroid.
One will be able to view, to take in my bestiary. My faith

will have become a mitre. Smoke, from the sculpting
of stone; bouquets, arboreal, crystals among lexicons;

one will see kamacite, falling. These chords,
geometries without space, this configuration of mind

will be learned, understood. It will be understood how
I have lost my mind. It will be understood why

my mind is not here. All languages will run dry, shrivel.
Desiccated minds, all. Man's figurations

levelled, deflated: sucked dry by arid aroliums. This
lubricant membrane, caustic, will continue to float

through the air; melancholic, tactile, miasmatic.

XIII

Uncovered – I will no longer have the need of speech.

Notes

Lutèce, Te Amo.

This sequence of poems – each corresponding by its number to the respective arrondissement of Paris – is much indebted to the photographs of Brassaï, Édouard Boubat and Robert Doisneau, particularly as they appear in the books:

> Édouard Boubat, *Amoureux de Paris* (Paris: Hors Collection, 1993).
> Brassaï, *Paris de nuit*, ed. by Paul Morand (Paris: Arts et métiers graphiques, 1987).
> Robert Doisneau, *Doisneau: Paris* (Paris: Flammarion, 2006).

The poems also owe a debt to Eric Hazan's *The Invention of Paris: A History in Footsteps* (London: Verso, 2010), while 'Sheer' would have been impossible without the exhibition *Portraits d'écrivains* (Paris: Maison Victor Hugo, 2010) and the photographs of Antonin Artaud by Denise Colomb and Henrie Martinie exhibited therein.

I should mention my obvious debt to the 2006 film *Paris, Je t'aime*, as well as my continuing debt to my partner, Eleanor Irving, with whom the topology of this sequence is a joint venture.

Hello London

1.6. See Louis MacNeice, 'Goodbye to London', in *The Burning Perch*.

Metousiosis

[*L'avocat*, 1866]
> Paul Cézanne, *L'avocat* (Oil on canvas, 1866).

[*Sitzender männlicher Akt*, 1910]
> Egon Schiele, *Sitzender männlicher Akt* (Oil on canvas, 1910).

1.1. 'Banishment, or the shedding blood for blood.
This stain of blood makes shipwreck of our state.'
> (Sophocles, *Oedipus Tyrannus*)

1.2. '... Così tra questa
Immensità s'annega il pensier mio:
E'l naufragar m'è dolce in questo mare.'
> (Giacomo Leopardi, *L'infinito*)

l.11. '... sum igitur praecise tantùm res cogitans, id est, mens, sive animus, sive intellectus, sive ratio, voces mihi priùs significationis ignotae. Sum autem res vera, & vere existens; sed qualis res? Dixi, cogitans...' (René Descartes, *Meditationes de Prima Philosophia*)

[*Le boeuf écorché*, 1924]
   Chaïm Soutine, *Le boeuf écorché* (Oil on canvas, 1924).
l.4. 'And the Word was made flesh, and dwelt among us...' (John I:14)

[*1947-J*, 1947]
   Clyfford Still, *1947-J* (Oil on canvas, 1947).
See Charles Baudelaire, 'Une Charogne', in *Les Fleurs du mal.*

[*Study after Vélazquez's Portrait of Pope Innocent X*, 1953]
   Francis Bacon, *Study after Vélazquez's Portrait of Pope Innocent X* (Oil on canvas, 1953).
l.12-13. See Melvyn Bragg's infamous *South Bank Show* interviews with Francis Bacon.

[*Head of J.Y.M. II*, 1984-85]
   Frank Auerbach, *Head of J.Y.M. II* (Oil on canvas, 1984-85).
l.10 'As his father
ran to escape him, Haemon failed to strike him,
and the poor wretch in anger at himself
leaned on his sword [ἔγχος] and drove it halfway in,
into his ribs [πλευραῖς].'
   (Sophocles, *Antigone.*)

[*Nice 'n easy*, 1999]
   John Currin, Nice 'n Easy, (Oil on Canvas, 1999).
l.7. 'fantasmatic'. See, for example, Lacan's fourteenth seminar: *La logique du fantasme* (1966-1967).

Paean pro Magna Societate

l.1-2. '... Turgot
takes a definition of the commonwealth
         for a definition of liberty.
Where ambition is every man's trade is no ploughing
How shall the plow be kept in the hands of owners not hirelings?'
   (Ezra Pound, *The Cantos*, LXVIII.)

'After

l.1-3. '... after great Lights, great Shadows are necessary, which he calls *Reposes*.' (John Dryden, *De Arte Graphica*).

Nervometer

This poem-sequence lurks somewhere between a version, collage and liberal translation of Antonin Artaud's *Le Pèse-Nerfs*.

L'Horloge

after Baudelaire

Clock! Sinister god – impassive, terrible – whose finger menaces: '*Remember!*
Misery, pulsing, will soon be shot into your fearful heart, as if a target;

pleasure, vapid, will vanish at the earth's edge, as the siren exits the stage;
each instant devours one tasty morsel of the human ration, our allotted pleasure.

Thirty-six hundred an hour, the seconds hush: *Remember!* – Quick,
insect voiced, say now: I am past, I suck your life with my grubby trunk.

Souviens-toi! Remember! Miser! Esto memor! [My metal larynx speaks all tongues].
The minutes, blithe mortal, are ore from which you must extract the results.

Remember that time is an inveterate gambler, winning without fail. It is the law.
The day declines; night grows. *Remember*, the void thirsts without end,
      clepsydra flows.

The hour, soon, will sound: divine chance, august virtue – your still-virginal
      spouse –
repentance even [that last respite!], all say: *death, old coward, it is too late!*'